# MEL BAY'
# EASIEST
# BANJO
## BOOK

### By William Bay & Neil Griffin

# Tuning the Banjo
## G – Bluegrass

The five strings are tuned to a piano as shown:

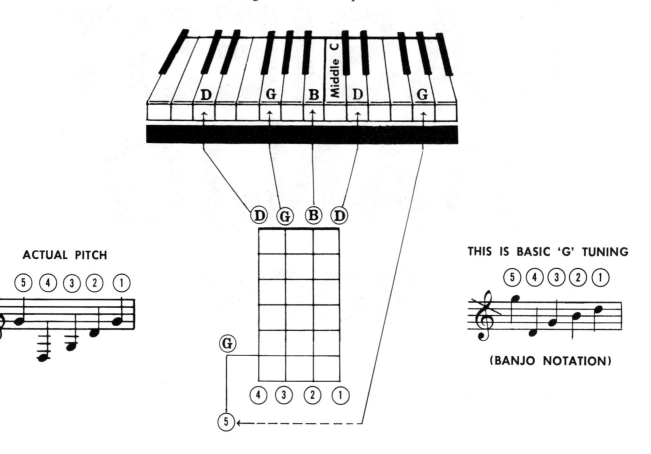

**ACTUAL PITCH**

**THIS IS BASIC 'G' TUNING**

**(BANJO NOTATION)**

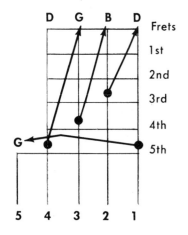

## ← Another Way to Tune

Tune the first string to D (next above middle C).

Tune the second string, noted at the 3rd fret, to the same pitch as the open first string.

Tune the third string, noted at the 4th fret, to the same pitch as the open second string.

Tune the fifth string to sound the same as the first string, noted at the 5th fret.

# Holding the Banjo

# Picks

Hold the pick in this manner, firmly between the thumb and first finger.

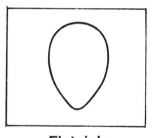

**Flatpick**

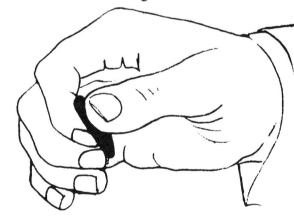

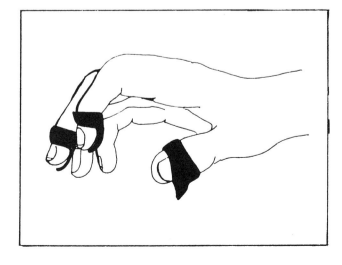

**Fingerpicks**

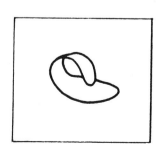

**Thumb Pick**

# Strumming

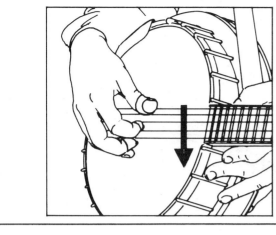

## Down Strum
/

Strum down across strings.

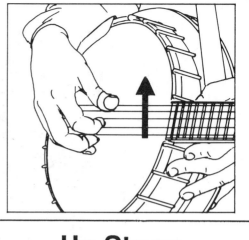

## Up Strum
V

Strum back up across strings.

# Chord Diagrams

A chord diagram is a drawing of the banjo neck. Hold the banjo in front of you so that you are facing the fingerboard. *The first string will be on your right.* Compare the banjo neck to the drawings below.

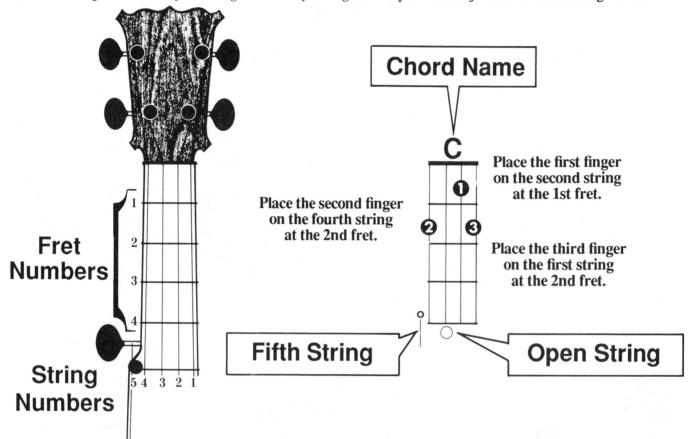

**Fret Numbers**

**String Numbers**

**Chord Name**

**C**

Place the first finger on the second string at the 1st fret.

Place the second finger on the fourth string at the 2nd fret.

Place the third finger on the first string at the 2nd fret.

**Fifth String**

**Open String**

An open circle under a string means that the string is to be played open. For example, in Figure 2, the third string is not touched by the fingers of the left hand. The third string is played, however.

A string marked with an "x" means that the sound of the string is to be deadened. The effect is the same as if the string was not played at all. For example, in the following D7 and F chords, the fifth string is not played.

4

# Basic Chords
## (Key of G)

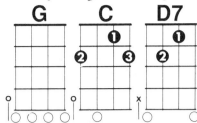

# Time Signatures

/ = down strum — from large string to small.

## $\frac{4}{4}$ or 𝄴 = Common Time
**4 strums or beats per measure.**

Hold the G chord and play it in this manner:

$\frac{4}{4}$  |G / / / / |G / / / / |G / / / / |G / / / /‖

## $\frac{3}{4}$ = Three-Four or Waltz Time
**3 strums or beats per measure.**

Hold the G chord and play it in the following manner:

$\frac{3}{4}$  |G / / / |G / / / |G / / / |G / / /‖

## $\frac{2}{4}$ = Two-Four Time
**2 strums or beats per measure.**

Play in the following manner:

$\frac{2}{4}$  |G / / |G / / |G / / |G / /‖

# Battle Hymn of the Republic

2. I have seen Him in the watch fires of a hundred circling camps.
                      C                    G           D7
They have builded Him an altar in the evening dews and damps.
         G
I have read His righteous sentence by the dim of flaring lamps,
         C     D7    G
His truth is marching on.

3. In the beauty of the lilies, Christ was born across the sea,
                      C                    G           D7
With a glory in His bosom that transfigures you and me;
         G
As He died to make men holy, Let us die to make men free,

         C     D7    G
While God is marching on.

# Bile 'Dem Cabbage Down

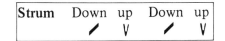

| Strum | Down | up | Down | up |
|-------|------|-----|------|-----|
|       | ╱    | V   | ╱    | V   |

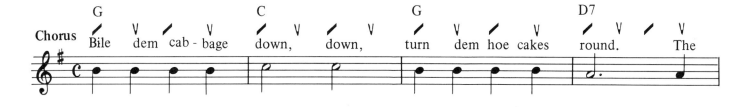

**Chorus** Bile dem cab-bage down, down, turn dem hoe cakes round. The

on-ly song that I can sing is bile dem Cab-bage down.

**Verse** 1. Went up on the moun-tain just to give my horn a blow,

thought I heard my true love say, "Yon-der comes my beau."

*Verses*

   G
2. Took my gal to the black-smith shop
           D7
   To have her mouth made small,
  G         C
   She turned around a time or two
     G    D7    G
   and swallowed shop and all.
  G             *Chorus*
3. Possum in a 'simmon tree,
   G         D7
   Raccoon on the ground,
   G           C
   Raccoon says, "You son-of-a-gun,
   G     D7   G
   Shake some 'simmons down!"
              *Chorus*

   G
4. Someone stole my old 'coon dog
           D7
   Wish they'd bring him back
  G         C
   He chased the big hogs thru the fence
    G    D7   G
   And the little ones thru the crack.
  G            *Chorus*
5. Met a possum in the road
           D7
   Blind as he could be,
  G         C
   Jumped the fence and whipped my dog.
    G  D7  G
   And bristled up at me.
           *Chorus*

   G
6. Once I had **an old gray mule,**
           D7
   His name was Siman Slick
   G       C
   He'd roll his eyes and back his ears,
   G    D7     G
   And how that mule would kick!
  G            *Chorus*
7. I've heard some folks tell **a tale**
           D7
   There's gold in them thar hills,
  G         C
   But I lived up there forty years
   G    D7     G
   And all I seen was stills!
            *Chorus*

# Away in a Manger

# This Little Light of Mine

# Peace Like a River

Strum: Down Down Down up Down up

1. I've got peace like a riv-er, I've got peace like a riv-er, I've got peace like a riv-er in my soul; I've got peace like a riv-er I've got peace like a riv-er, I've got peace like a riv-er in my soul.

2. I've got joy like a fountain

3. I've got love like an **ocean.**

# I Never Will Marry

Strum: Down Down Down up

I nev-er will mar-ry,_____ nor___ be no man's wife,_____ I ex-pect to stay sin-gle,_____ all the days of my life

Chorus: shells in the o-cean_____ will___ be my death bed;_____ The fish in deep wa-ter_____ swim o-ver my head.

1. life    The    2. head.

| G | D7 | G | C |

1. One day as I rambled down by the seashore,

| G | | D7 | G |

The wind it did whistle and the waters did roar.

| D7 | | G | C |

I spied a fair damsel make a pitiful cry,

| G | | D7 | G |

It sounded so lonesome in the waters nearby.

Chorus

| G | D7 | G | C |

2. My love's gone and left me, he's the one I adore,

| G | | D7 | G |

He's **gone** where I never shall see him any more.

| D7 | | G | C |

She plunged her dear body in the water so deep,

| G | | D7 | G |

She closed her pretty blue eyes in the waters to sleep.

Chorus

# Blow, Ye Winds

# The Wabash Cannonball

# She'll Be Coming Round the Mountain

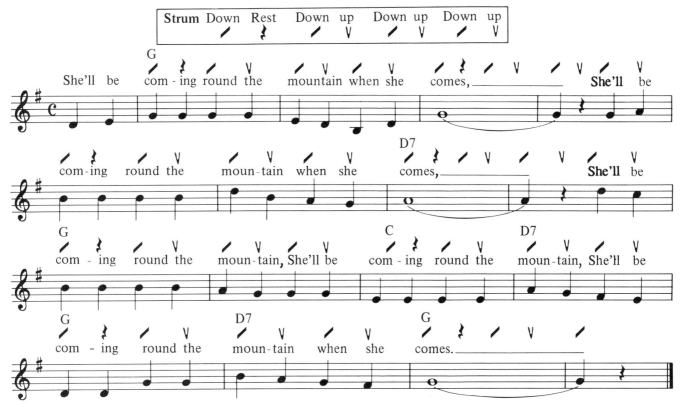

# The Gospel Train

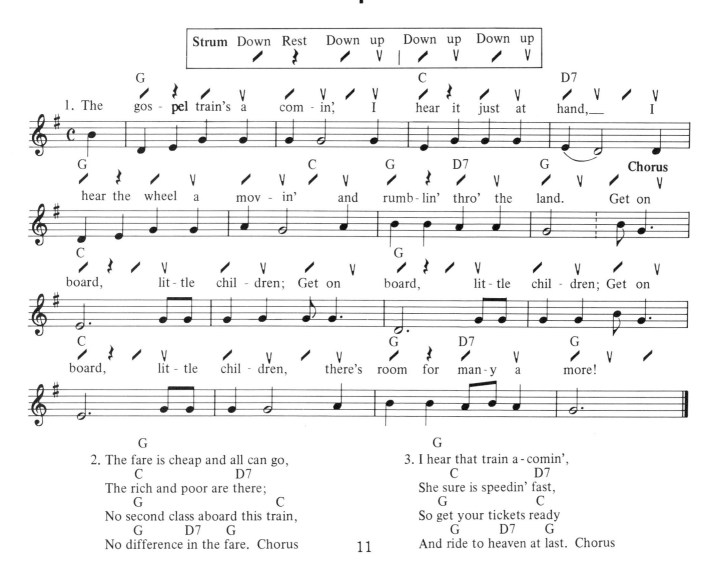

| | |
|---|---|
| G | G |
| 2. The fare is cheap and all can go, | 3. I hear that train a-comin', |
|   C          D7 |   C          D7 |
| The rich and poor are there; | She sure is speedin' fast, |
|  G              C |  G             C |
| No second class aboard this train, | So get your tickets ready |
|  G    D7  G |  G    D7  G |
| No difference in the fare. Chorus | And ride to heaven at last. Chorus |

# Down by the Riverside

2. I'm gonna join hands with everyone, etc.
3. I'm gonna put on my long white robe, etc.
4. I'm gonna talk with the **Prince of Peace, etc.**

12

# Tablature

Standard tablature is used as follows:

1st String
2nd String
3rd String
4th String
5th String

0 = open string
1 = string pressed down on 1st fret
2 = string pressed down on 2nd fret
3 = string pressed down on 3rd fret
etc.

The chart below shows all of the notes on the first few frets of the banjo. The top line shows the notes in standard musical notation. The names of the notes are in the middle. The bottom line shows the notes in tablature.

# Counting Time in Tablature

The top number of the time signature tells how many counts per measure.

4 counts per measure          3 counts per measure

Measure          Measure          Measure          Measure

In over 90% of all three-finger banjo picking, there is one, two, or three notes (sounds) to each count of the music. Here are examples of how they are counted:

Tap your foot *once* for each count of the measure and play one, two, or three notes on each tap as shown in the tablature....

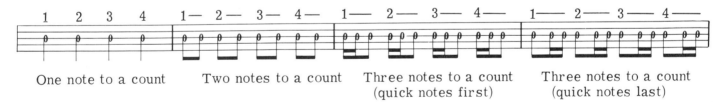

One note to a count          Two notes to a count          Three notes to a count (quick notes first)          Three notes to a count (quick notes last)

♩ This is a one-count rest (period of silence for one tap).
A dot ( · ) adds one half count to a tone = 1 ½ counts:

If a note is to be held longer than one count, the first count will have the regular stem, and an additional stem will be added for each extra count.

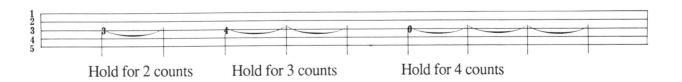

Hold for 2 counts          Hold for 3 counts          Hold for 4 counts

13

# Basic Banjo Picking Effects

The three effects that are most used in banjo playing are explained below. Practice them over and over until each is clear sounding and even. The string is picked only once, but two separate notes are sounded. Always pick the first note a little harder when *sliding, hammering,* or *pulling-off* so that both notes are heard clearly before the sound dies away.

## The Slide (SL)

Pick the first note of each slide in the normal way. Then, keeping the left-hand finger pressed firmly down, slide quickly to the second note which is found in the fret shown in the tablature. The second finger of the left hand is used to finger most slides because of its strength.

## The Hammer (H)

Pick the first note of each hammer in the normal way. To obtain the second note, tap the left-hand finger down hard and fast onto the string from about an inch above the fingerboard. Hammering right behind a fret gives the clearest and loudest sound.

## The Pull-Off (P)

Pick the first note of each pull-off in the normal way. To obtain the second note, use the left-hand finger you are pushing down with to "pluck" or pick the string in a downward direction. The sound will be clearer if you keep pressure on the string as you pull-off the left-hand finger.

## Left-Hand Fingering

The first finger presses down notes on the 1st fret.

The second finger presses down notes on the 2nd fret.

The third finger presses down notes on the 3rd fret.

The fourth finger presses down notes on the 4th fret.

## Right-Hand Fingering

Correct right-hand fingering for picking is indicated under the notes as follows:

T = Pick with thumb (down)
I = Pick with index finger (up)
M = Pick with middle finger (up)

If fingering is not shown, use the middle finger for the first string, the index finger for the second string, and the thumb for the third, fourth, and fifth strings.

H = Hammer
SL = Slide
P = Pull-Off

## Sourwood Mountain

Arr. by Neil Griffin

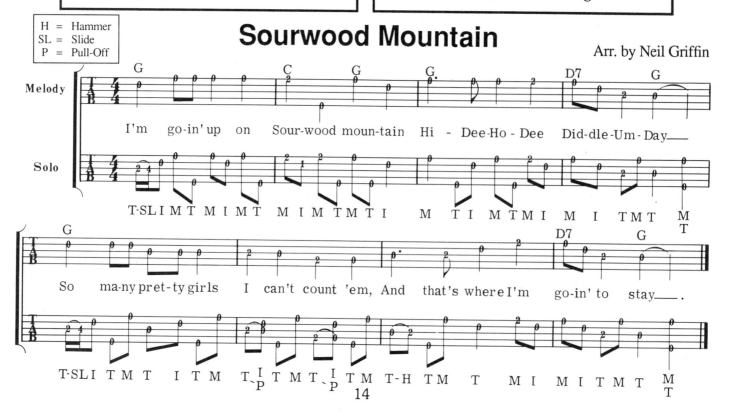

14

# Amazing Grace

H = Hammer
SL = Slide
P = Pull-Off

Arr. by Neil Griffin

15

# Cider Through a Straw

Arr. by Neil Griffin

16

# I'm Gonna Sing When the Spirit Says Sing

Arr. by Neil Griffin

# He's Got the Whole World in His Hands

Arr. by Neil Griffin

# Down in the Valley

Arr. by Neil Griffin

# Michael, Row the Boat Ashore

Arr. by Neil Griffin

# Goin' Down the Road Feelin' Bad

Arr. by Neil Griffin

# I'm on My Way

Arr. by Neil Griffin

# No Hiding Place

Arr. by Neil Griffin

# Our Boys Will Shine Tonight

Arr. by Neil Griffin

# Banjo Chord Reference Chart
## The Major Chords

○ = (5th String Open)

### (C)
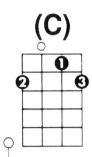

### F
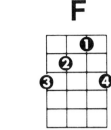

### B♭
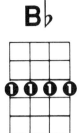

### E♭
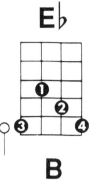

### A♭
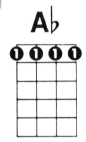

### D♭
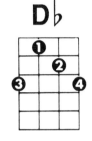

### G♭/F♯
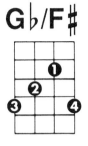

### B
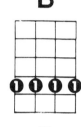

### E
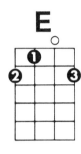

### A
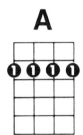

### D
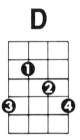

### G
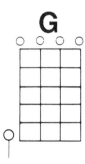

## The Minor Chords

### Cm
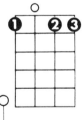

### Fm
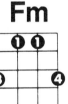

### B♭m
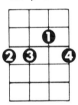

### E♭m
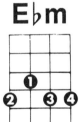

### A♭m
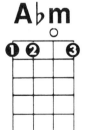

### D♭m
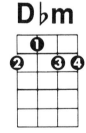

### G♭m/F♯m
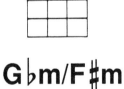

### Bm
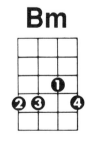

### Em
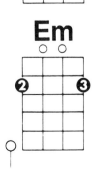

### Am
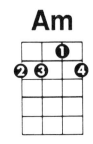

### Dm
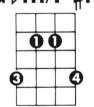

### Gm
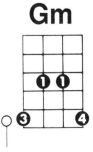

23

# The Seventh Chords
## (7 = Seventh)

### C7
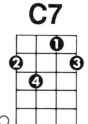

### F7
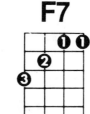

### B♭7
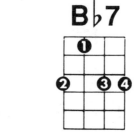

### E♭7
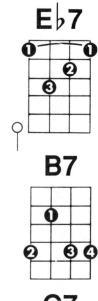

### A♭7
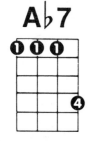

### D♭7
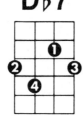

### G♭7/F♯7
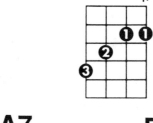

### B7

### E7
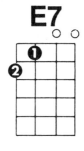

### A7
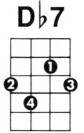

### A7
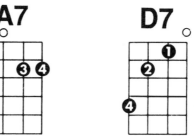

### D7
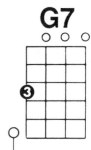

### G7

# The Diminished Chords
## (– = Diminished)

### F-  A♭-
### B-  D-
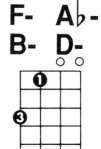

### C-  E♭-
### F♯-  A-

### G-  B♭
### C♯-  E-
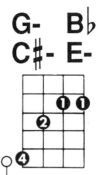

# The Augmented Chords
## (+ = Augmented)

### E♭+
### G+ B+
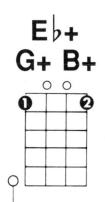

### E+
### A♭+ C+

### F+  A+
### C♯+  D♭+

### G♭+ F♯+
### B♭  D+
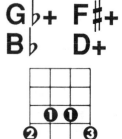